Find your
CALLING

DISCOVERING WHAT YOU'RE MEANT TO DO: A 21-DAY GUIDE FOR HER

BY VERONICA & DALE PARTRIDGE

StartupCamp.com a DBA of Dale Partridge, Inc.
70 S.W. Century Drive. #100-503
Bend, Oregon 97702
www.StartupCamp.com

Ordering Information:
Quantity sales. Special discounts are available on quantity purchases by corporations, associations, and others. For details, contact the publisher at the address above or by email at support@startupcamp.com

Printed in the United States of America

Category: Self-Help
Partridge, Dale.
Find Your Calling : Discovering What You're Meant To Do: A 21-Day Guide For Her / Veronica and Dale Partridge

ISBN-13: 978-0692803523

First Edition

TABLE OF CONTENTS

00: OUR STORY

Several years ago I (Dale) was devastated when a friend I admired leaned across the dinner table and called me the B-word. No, not that one. He called me "busy."

"You do a lot of stuff, Dale. You always have new projects and new ideas," he said. "But you seem scattered... almost like you don't know what you're meant to do. So, I'm just going to ask you, do you?"

His bold question caught me off-guard and I froze.

I fumbled my way through the rest of our conversation, defending myself and my schedule. I threw out convoluted reasons for my muddled mess of a pursuit.

I left the dinner table that night embarrassed and convicted about not having a clear answer to his question.

In that moment, though, I decided to put to death my aimless aspirations and abandon the purposeless life where many find themselves trapped. Ultimately, my friend's query sent me on a journey to discover my calling, and that journey has been one of the most rewarding of my life.

I (Veronica) have seen the success in Dale's life that's resulted from the journey to discover his calling. Now seeing him live out his unique purpose has inspired me to more fully embrace mine. For the season of life that I'm in, that drove me to creating a home where everyone in our family can thrive. But I'd like to think I'm more complex than that; I'm also passionate about engaging the larger cultural conversation around the value of children and the fight to protect women against domestic violence. Ultimately, what I'm learning is as both Dale and I embrace our unique callings, we are becoming the people we were created to be.

What about you? Are you a woman living the kind of 'reactive' life that Dale's friend exposed to him—never making steps toward an identified destination? Do you just respond to whatever is presented to you?

6

Most women I know feel a lot of pressure to do it all. We're expected to succeed in the workplace, have a great marriage, raise children, look fantastic—and make it all look effortless! The myth we've believed is that doing it all is better than living out our unique callings. But Dale and I want you to know that there is a path for you that actually is better than juggling all the looks that women today are expected to present. What's even better is to live out the calling that is uniquely yours.

We've always defined calling as a mountaintop destination that can only be discovered by you. It's found as you develop your natural gifts and it culminates in the realization of your life's greatest work. It's a journey that allows women to feel vibrant, meaningful, and important.

We believe every woman, including you, has a unique calling—though most haven't found theirs. While it's not impossible to identify, it can be difficult to discover. We have to work to find and unleash it.

I (Dale) wish I could tell you that after my friend confronted me about my distracted pursuits, I discovered my calling the next day and my life has been sensational ever since. But the conversation only launched a frustrating journey in which I explored a variety of different routes leading only to dead-end streets and quick-turn cul-de-sacs. Along the way

Veronica and I discovered a series of principles and practices that clarified my calling and can help you discover yours.

This book is a field guide to help women move from a busy life—where women are bullied daily into managing all that others expect of them—to a called one. While the information is arranged in 21 chronological days, you don't have to complete the journey in three quick weeks. Take your time and don't be afraid to return to one of the day's entries if you need to spend more time with it. This process shouldn't be hurried. Purpose to stay focused so that you don't miss, misread, or confuse what you're learning about your unique calling.

Although this book is short, it isn't easy. We're asking you to make uncomfortable choices and difficult decisions. If you're looking for a quick painless process to live a life of meaning, this book is not for you. This book demands maturity. It insists on your understanding the difference between 'should' and 'could,' 'smart' and 'right.' Veronica and I both challenge you not to allow what you want to do to prevent what you're meant to do.

Furthermore, this book unfolds progressively. Like the movement toward your calling, it gets better as you get further into it! The lessons dive deeper, the activities reveal more, and the implications become evident.

Avoid speed-reading or shortcuts. Trust the map and trust the guide.

Believe us when we say this, women: living without a clear sense of calling is a prison sentence. But unlike physical prisons, you can leave any time. Now is the time to break out of the cell of busyness and leave the valley of reactive living.

Follow us to freedom.
Follow us to the mountain top.

Veronica & Dale Partridge

NOTES FOR THOUGHTS

"The two most important days in your life are the day you are born and the day you find out why."

MARK TWAIN

#FindYourCalling

DAY 01
It Comes At A Cost

You're talented. Maybe people have told you that
before—a teacher or neighbor or your parents. You're
also passionate. People sense it in conversation
with you around certain topics. Maybe friends have
complimented how kind and empathetic and passionate
you can be.

As you notice your talent, passion, and desire for more,
you are wondering if you have a calling.

As I mentioned earlier, the answer is 'yes.' I know this
because you're reading this book. Deep down in your
gut, something big is stirring. You may not know where
it comes from or what it wants you to do, but you can't

deny that it exists. This almost divine dissatisfaction is triggered by—you guessed it—your calling. And the task before you is to not just discover it, but to live it.

If you have a pulse, you have a purpose. If you are breathing, you are meant for meaning. If you doubt whether you have a calling, you need only to believe three truths for now.

What you feel is normal. This stirring is universal among women. Although this yearning for meaning may or may not have been encouraged by those around you when you were young, and may or may not be affirmed now, what you're noticing is natural. It's how you're wired. The impulse to discover a larger purpose is how you were made.

What you feel is positive. This impulse toward more doesn't mean you're inherently dissatisfied or psychologically imbalanced. It means you want to do something meaningful with your life. In fact, this yearning can be the catapult that propels you toward purpose. So don't resist this feeling; embrace it. The degree to which we listen to and act on the things which drive us determines how much fulfillment we will experience.

What you feel is impermanent. If the deep, hungry stirring makes you miserable, take hope. Millions of women have gone before you and they have broken through to the other side. You will not be purposeless forever. In order to move forward, you must believe this: Calling comes at a cost, and it's expensive. Not in dollars, but in emotional bandwidth.

Merriam-Webster defines a 'calling' as "a strong inner impulse toward a particular course of action especially when accompanied by conviction of divine influence." If you feel an inner impulse toward a new course of action, take a deep breath. The conviction of divine influence and a better life may be right around the corner.

ASK

When did I first notice a stirring to accomplish something more? Are there any associations I connect with this feeling that could shed more light on it?

_____

_____

_____

_____

_____

_____

_____

_____

_____

BELIEVE

My calling is expensive. I will make the payments with time, acute attentiveness, and emotional maturation.

DO   ☐ COMPLETED

Initiate an intentional 15-30 minute conversation about calling, and your journey to find yours, with your closest female friend.

"The only way
to support a
revolution is to
make your own."

SOPHIA AMORUSO

#FindYourCalling

DAY 02
Humans Love Rules

Humans love rules. Because a lot of us want others to remove the guesswork of living, we can allow others to tell us what to do. When we accept the rules of others, it allows us to escape the hard work of using discernment.

So, we're sorry to tell you that there isn't an ironclad three-step process that you must follow to discover your calling. Instead, you must learn to navigate the mystery of it all.

And even though calling is a mystery, it isn't a complete mystery. It exists within a rough structure that can help guide us through the process of identifying what we're meant to do.

The framework begins with a counterintuitive principle: Calling is a singular word, but it is a plural principle. In other words, we often talk about 'calling,' but it might be more accurate to discuss 'callings.'

Primary calling

Your primary calling is your heart's song. It's the song playing in your brain all the time. This is more than a job. It's more than a career path. It's more than a task list. Your primary calling is your life's soundtrack; the thoughts and actions that circle around it consume you.

Secondary calling

Your secondary calling is your hand's work. It's the expression of your gifting that often occupies your time. You might get paid to live out your secondary calling, and it can change over time. It's an activity that may flow from your natural gifting and helps prepare you for your primary calling, yet it lives outside of its epicenter.

Our friend Audrey, who recently turned 25, launched a marriage ministry called "Beating50Percent.com.com." Convinced that every marriage has a unique purpose that requires intentional commitment, her blog is inviting millions of wives to create the marriage they desire. It has been a delight to watch her embrace this important work. As she's gathered more mature women around her, we've seen Audrey blossom as she cultivates the gifts she's been given and lives out her purpose.

Because Audrey is at the trailhead at the base of the mountain, we don't know exactly where her journey will take her. But we do know that, in whatever way it unfolds, her calling will continue to be one in which she's using her gifts and blessing others. The work of her hands is her secondary calling and while her "day job," might change over the years, her heart will continue to play the same song.

The first task in the journey toward your calling is to listen to your life. What is the song playing in the background throughout your day? Your calling is familiar, but it may not be obvious. So take time to reflect and listen for the melody. Do you hear it?

ASK

What do I love learning about, talking about, or
teaching about?

_____

_____

_____

_____

_____

_____

BELIEVE

To fulfill my primary calling I must operate daily in my
secondary calling.

DO   ☐ COMPLETED

List 5 possible life paths that require the use of your
natural giftings.

_____

_____

_____

_____

_____

"Know yourself.
Because
you can't fix
something
you don't
understand."

#FindYourCalling

DAY 03
Calling Never Compromises

Most leaders I (Dale) know reveal that core values are important to their businesses. Most have defined them and many discuss them regularly in team meetings, but when I ask these leaders about their personal values, they often stammer, stutter, and grow silent. Just as a company cannot accomplish its mission without clearly understanding its values, so you cannot uncover your calling if you don't know what guides you.

Whether you're running a business, completing grad work, managing a home, or punching a timecard, it's critical to identify what you value most.

I (Veronica) value relationships. But it's not that I

value a breadth of relationships; I don't need to have 300 people in my phone contacts. Rather, I value depth of relationship. And depth can't happen in relationship without authenticity. Genuine relationship isn't possible with people who are wearing masks to give the appearance that their life is better than it is. Because I'm convinced that vulnerability breeds healthy relationships, vulnerability is a value that I purpose to live out in my own life.

What do you value more than anything else in life? What determines your moral code? What do you refuse to give up, no matter the stakes? What are your non-negotiables?

While you may be tempted to believe that your values are separate from your calling, the two are inextricably connected. Calling tends to flow from your beliefs and intersects with everything you do.

Your calling will complement rather than compete with your values and priorities.

For example, if you value healthy family relationships and your sense of 'calling' would weaken your relationships with them, you haven't identified it. If your 'calling' requires you to do harm to your reputation, then you need to rethink it. If your 'calling' leads you to take on an irresponsible amount of debt, then you have likely missed the mark.

Your calling should fit your life like a good pair of shoes. If you're a size 8, you won't try to squeeze into a 5 (Don't buy the hype either... I wear a 5 and can NEVER find shoes). If you're training for a marathon, you're not going to wear those sexy heels tucked in your closet! You're going to wear the most comfy pair of running shoes you can find. This isn't to say that you won't have to break them in before you hit your stride. You will! You might even need a shoehorn to slide into the shoes you're meant to wear. But, ultimately, they'll fit your feet and get you where you're going. Resistance is healthy; incompatibility should be an alarm. You never need to compromise what you believe to live out what you were meant to do. And a woman is more likely to compromise her values if she hasn't defined them yet.

ASK

What areas of my life do I believe are worth protecting
and why?

_____

_____

_____

_____

_____

BELIEVE

My calling will complement my values, not compromise
them.

DO   ☐ COMPLETED

Define your five personal core values. List them as short
phrases with one sentence to support each.

_____

_____

_____

_____

_____

_____

_____

"It's not hard to make decisions once you know what your values are."

ROY E. DISNEY

#FindYourCalling

DAY 04
The Questions Behind
The Questions

When you and your spouse or roommate meet at home at the end of the day, one of you asks, "What should we have for dinner?" You could respond to the question with whatever comes to your mind, but your answer is meaningless if you haven't answered other questions first.

For example you have to ask, "Which ingredients do we have?" You may want a pot roast, but if all you have is flour and sunflower seeds, don't waste time firing up the crockpot. You're not having roast. You also need to ask, "What food restrictions do we have?" If you make that pot roast for your vegetarian roomie or bake a loaf of bread while you and your spouse are on the Paleo diet, dinner isn't going to be a hit.

Some of the most mundane and the most significant questions in life are predicated on other questions. And so it is with your calling. That's why we always suggest that women who are searching for their calling begin by asking the questions behind the question. Here are three critical questions to answer before you'll ever discern your calling.

Do I believe in God?

Twentieth century author A.W. Tozer once said, "What comes into our minds when we think about God is the most important thing about us." He's right. And what you believe about God will influence what you think about calling: whether it exists, where it comes from, and what you must do to discover it. For some of you, the very question causes jaded skepticism and memories of unfortunate Sunday school experiences to bubble up in your gut. Don't skip this one. It must be defined by yes or no in order to move forward.

Do I want to be married?

If you want to live out your calling in society, you'll need to determine how you want to be engaged with society. The primary way most people throughout history have engaged with culture is through marriage and family. Of course, marriage isn't for everyone. But, historically and statistically, it's for most people. If you don't have a desire for marriage, you should ask yourself why. A firm yes or no answer to this question will help you be intentional about connecting to the world and others in distinct ways. And while you can't manipulate when marriage happens, noticing it as the desire of your heart is a helpful indicator on this journey.

Do I want children?

Our modern culture paints the birth and rearing of children as being expensive and inconvenient. However, we both believe that children help women and help men become who we were made to be. For a lot of guys, fatherhood becomes the entry point to maturity. For a lot of women, motherhood offers the satisfaction of doing what women's bodies were designed to do. We both believe that children are a good gift. That's not to say that it's not hard work. It is! Children will influence where you live, how you live, and what you can and can't do in any given season of life. But for women called to motherhood—and if you have kids, you can assume you're called to it!—it can be one of the most satisfying jobs you'll ever do. Children will transform you into a version of yourself you cannot develop any other way.

Your life is largely a function of the clarity you've chosen for yourself. So, you need to determine not only the macro structure of your life—faith, marriage, children—but also the level of organizational clarity you desire. Next, you must embrace and cultivate the behaviors that prepare you for what you're meant to do.

You need to build a life that invites calling in.

It's difficult to invite calling into chaos. Do you still struggle to get up on time in the morning? Do you wrestle to keep your house clean? Do you run late to appointments or under-deliver on expectations? How can you expect to excavate your life's purpose while you're still a girl who's waiting for her mom to wake her up for school and make her lunch?

You can't play in the yard if you won't get off the fence. And you can't live your calling if you refuse to make decisions. The recent generation's dilemmas of doubt, indecision, and fear of commitment will shipwreck your journey toward discovering your calling before it even begins. So, look in the mirror, grow up, and answer the questions behind the questions.

ASK

If something is holding me back from answering the three questions behind the questions, what is it? If not, what is it that keeps me committed to these choices?

_____

_____

_____

_____

_____

_____

_____

_____

BELIEVE

I can't find my calling until I find the answers to my life's biggest questions.

DO   ☐ COMPLETED

Set aside 60-90 minutes to evaluate these three questions. Do research if you need to, have an important conversation, or confront difficult thoughts. Stick with it until your answers leave you with a settled conviction on where you stand. If you notice that your decision—to be married or to have children—is contingent on someone else, acknowledge this and release it into God's care.

NOTES FOR THOUGHTS

"The middle way
is no way."

ABIGAIL ADAMS

DAY 05
Let The Right Ones In

I (Veronica) have noticed that men and women naturally approach our journeys to discover our callings a bit differently. A lot of guys assume their calling is something they have to discover alone, and they also see it as something that only relates to their jobs.

This is actually really interesting. Where men's vision for their lives can be more macular, women are often able to keep a wider range of needs and people and options in view. In discussing physical vision, doctors of history trace differences between men and women's physical vision back to the way of life 8,000-10,000 years ago. They say, "Naturally, women have better peripheral vision because they gathered food for their families.

Men have much stronger straight-on vision for hunting purposes."[1] Fascinating, right?

Many people think about calling as a personal decision that impacts their professional roles. But we've already learned that calling is not just a professional matter. Today, we'll also notice that discerning it is not solely personal.

In the words of the poet John Donne, "No man is an island, entire of itself; every man is a piece of a continent, a part of the main."[2] Women, too! Each of us must rely on those around us. This is true of almost every aspect of our lives, especially our callings.

When Dale speaks to men, he challenges them, "You don't get to do this alone." And I'd add, "You don't have to do this alone." On this particular journey, independence is your enemy. Finding your calling requires intentional community and intense conversation. It requires safe people you've allowed to speak into your life.

Calling is always connected to community. The search process requires the perspectives of others. I'd guess that you've had conversations about your future with your girlfriends or sisters. You might not have identified it as "calling," but that's what you would have been imagining as you dreamed of what your future might hold. If you

haven't, this is your opportunity! Ask the women who
know you best, both peers and mentors, where they
see you excelling. Ask them where they recognize that
which makes you come alive. Ask them where they
notice your fiery passions finding expression. But most
importantly, allow women to provide an honest view of
you as you navigate your voyage.

Because calling is not only professional, you can expect
this process to get personal. What you're doing is a
radical act of vulnerability. So the people you invite into
this conversation matter. They need to be safe, wise, and
committed to your flourishing. Ideally, they have history
with you. In other words, don't ask your co-worker who
you don't spend time with or the girl you met at the
gym last month. If they haven't walked deeply with you
before today, they shouldn't walk with you through this.

And because calling is both personal and professional,
look for individuals who share similar giftings to yours.
Consider people who have success in an area you'd like
to explore. If you imagine a career, meet with a woman
who's working pursuing hers outside or inside the home.
If you see children in your future, by birth or adoption,
talk to other moms. If you can identify the type of work
you'd like to be doing, connect with a woman in that
field. Find people whose life is ordered, settled, and
directed. If you don't respect them both personally and
professionally, their advice won't move you.

Your calling is not just about what's smart for you. It's about what's right for you.

Having the ability to determine the difference between what's smart—because it's strategic or lucrative—and what's right, the unique calling that has your name on it, is critical as you choose your team of advisors.

To make this even trickier, you must be capable of defining what 'right' is. For example, in philosophy, the word 'ought' has an implied moral authority. It suggests a universal right and wrong. In other words, phrases like 'should', 'ought', and 'right' are much weightier than we might realize.

We're both Christians. That means the Bible is the foundational moral compass that guides us. We're not preaching at you, but we mention that to alert you to the need for a stable, unchanging ground from which you can determine 'right' and 'wrong.' As a great writer once said:

"When the storm has swept by, the unfounded are gone but the firm stand forever." - Proverbs 10:25

There are plenty of worthy paths on the journey to discern your calling. There are many smart people to help you find the way, but in order to discover the right path, you'll need to surround yourself with the right people. You'll need to know what 'right' truly is. It's a deep question, and a critical one. Calling can't be discovered by a woman who has a moving target of morality.

ASK

How do I determine right and wrong? Is it my government, my culture, my faith, or something else? Does it ever change? If so, why?

_____

_____

_____

_____

_____

_____

_____

BELIEVE

My calling is found through right thinking, not smart thinking.

DO   ☐ COMPLETED

List 1 to 3 safe, right people you'll ask for outside perspective this week.

_____

_____

_____

_____

"Just because
something is
smart, doesn't
mean it's right."

UNKNOWN

DAY 06
Own It

We've mentioned the importance of making wise choices in this process, but calling requires both choices and change. And change is where most of us get stuck.

A few days ago, we discussed the three major questions to answer before tackling the other questions. If you believe in God, what changes? If you want to be married, what changes? If you want to have kids, what changes?

Change is derived from a shift in thinking. New thinking results in new behaviors. New behaviors produce different outcomes.

Backing up a bit, these changes are behaviors that are often identified more commonly as: personal habits, discipline, routine, and schedule. These are where clarity begins. They're where your life comes into focus.

I (Veronica) am convinced that creating and keeping a daily routine is what allows people and families to thrive. For me, I've established a predictable structure that allows our children to grow and learn and eat and rest—and even get daily playtime with Dale and I. It's also great for me. I know that when kids are napping, I can accomplish what I need to and even tend to my passions by listening to an audiobook or writing an article on my blog. It also means that I can anticipate getting my tank refilled through quality time with Dale or with our close friends over a glass of wine.

The less time I spent wondering what to do with my day, the more time I had to determine what I could do with my life.

The process of finding our callings isn't all that complicated. We make it complicated because of our fear to commit to the things we've said we will do, follow the direction we know we should go, and embrace the life we have chosen to create. A called woman will not allow fear of overcoming the discrepancy between who she is now and who she is meant to become to hinder her.

So, beat back the procrastination, clarify what two or three major things must change, and implement the necessary habits and structure that will allow your calling to reveal itself to you.

ASK

What two or three major things in my life need to
change to welcome calling into my life?

_____

_____

_____

_____

_____

_____

BELIEVE

Choices and change are different. My calling requires
both.

DO   ☐ COMPLETED

From your answers above, list the daily habits or routine
adjustments you will make to support these changes.

_____

_____

_____

_____

_____

_____

"Instead of wishing things would change, ask God for the strength to make a change."

LYSA TERKEURST

DAY 07
The Career Of Calling

'Calling' has been so overused in recent years that it has morphed into something of a catch-all junk drawer for how we spend our time. Do you like to knit? Great, that's your calling. Do you sell insurance to make ends meet? Excellent, you've found your calling! Have you been doing interior design for 25 years? Fantastic, that must be your calling.

To be honest, most of us have a better idea of what we don't want in a job than what we do want. We don't want something mundane. We don't want anything similar to the work of our parents who took temperatures or worked in cubicles. And we certainly don't want anything with a two-hour commute. After all, a third of our lives will be spent working. We'll probably spend more time at work than we do with our spouses and kids. It's no wonder we agonize over 'what to be when we grow up.'

We want a job that doesn't actually feel like a job. We hunger for something that uses our talents and brings us great satisfaction. What we really want isn't a job at all; we want a calling.

In order to understand what your calling is, you'll need to recognize what your calling is not. So, let's identify and eliminate four competing concepts that are not synonymous with calling.

Hobby

A hobby is something you do because you enjoy it. Or because it fascinates you. Perhaps you do it because it just passes the time. Hobbies don't stress you out. Typically, they relax you. I (Veronica) enjoy being with animals and I love to make macramé wall hangings. Maybe you like to kayak on the river or write fiction novels, or maybe you're a fitness freak who goes to the gym three hours a day. Dale and some of his friends are obsessed with their knives. They fiddle with them constantly, opening them and closing them. Honestly, I don't get it. But if that's your thing, go for it. You rarely get paid for your hobby, and if you do, it usually ceases to be a hobby.

Job

If you're married with children, your husband might provide the family's income, or you might both work. If you're single, and you're not a Hilton or a Trump, you're going to have to have a job. This is what pays the bills. You may or may not enjoy it. You may or may not be paid well to do it, but you have this job because it allows you to survive in a capitalistic society. When you leave your job for the day, you usually stop thinking about it unless you're lucky enough to have an overbearing boss who doesn't understand boundaries. In today's marketplace, few jobs offer lasting security and stability. In fact, yours will likely change 15 to 20 times in your lifetime.[3]

Career

"Career" is the word most commonly used to describe the long arc of someone's employment. The word derives from the medieval Latin word *carraria*, which means "road for vehicles." This is the path you take through a series of jobs over time and it is usually associated with a single occupation. If you're in your thirties or older, you may be on a career path by now.

Calling

Calling is often used interchangeably with vocation, which comes from the Latin word meaning "to call." Your calling is the pursuit that gives you meaning. It's the rumble in your gut. It's the way you would orient your life to accomplish what matters most if you found out you had a terminal illness. I (Dale) wish I'd heard when I was younger that one's calling is not something to be magically revealed, but is something to be recognized.

You have to listen for it. You have to search for it. You have to discover it, even as it discovers you. Of the four ways to think about how you glean meaning and purpose and sustenance, calling is the only one that you can expect to remain consistent over a lifetime.

When it comes to lasting satisfaction and happiness, those who occupy themselves with hobbies and jobs are the least satisfied.[4] Those who pursue career and calling feel the most satisfied. No surprises there. As I've clarified, your calling encompasses more than the work you are paid for; it taps into your whole life purpose. When you've found your calling, you experience satisfaction and genuine fulfillment. Conversely, if you're living a life at odds with your vocation, the fruitlessness of that choice will be evident as well. You may be indescribably restless. Or maybe you wake up in the middle of the night feeling like you can't breathe. Life may seem to be passing you by.

Unfortunately, as we get older, our true selves can get lost among the influences and expectations of family, friends, teachers, and the media. In school and in society we get sorted and placed into labeled slots. Instead of listening to the call within us, we begin to make decisions based on our need for security or approval.

Embracing your calling means rejecting the misguided voices of others and choosing to live authentically. It means refusing to blindly imitate your mom or other women you admire. Too often we heed every voice, influence, and belief except our own. We drink up what our teachers tell us, what our parents tell us, what our ministers tell us, and what other wise sages have spoken and written. We make these sources of truth authoritative, but we dismiss our own insights and understanding as hopelessly irrelevant.[5]

Your hobbies won't likely stem from your calling. Your job may not be connected to your calling. Your career may not be an extension of your calling, but, ideally, that's the goal. If you've been confusing your calling with its cousins, it's time to change your thinking. If you can, you'll be one step closer to discovering what you are meant to do.

ASK

Is my job supporting my passions or smothering them?
What changes can I make this month that will help
develop me for what I'm meant to do?

_____

_____

_____

_____

_____

BELIEVE

I can't discover my calling if I confuse it with career, job,
or hobbies.

DO   ☐ COMPLETED

Below, list your hobbies, your job, and your career path.
Then draft a description of what you're beginning to
discern that your calling might be. .

_____

_____

_____

_____

_____

_____

"The deepest vocational question is not 'What ought I to do with my life?' It is the more demanding 'Who am I?' What is my nature?'"

PARKER J. PALMER

DAY 08
Calling Is Never For You

As I (Veronica) mentioned, a lot of men have a 'me'-centric, or myopic, understanding of calling. They believe that finding their calling will make them more fulfilled, more productive, more successful, more happy and more wealthy. They don't always give much thought to how others could and should be affected.

As Dale was on that journey to discover his calling, he founded an ecommerce company with a simple mission. The company sold high-quality goods and donated a portion of each purchase to a charitable organization. He enjoyed himself and felt the work he was doing was propelling him closer to what he was meant to do. One day a friend of his noticed the good that the organization had accomplished and mused, "Dang, Dale. Imagine if you didn't start this company."

His comment was a simple observation, but it struck a nerve for Dale. For the first time, he considered all the people whose lives would have been different if he'd said 'no' to that dream. If he'd chosen to avoid the pursuit he felt called to, it's possible that thousands of people might have died. Because the business funded fresh water wells, fed hungry children, and provided shelter to those in need, the millions of dollars they raised had very palpable life and death consequences.

Your calling is always about others.

So how will your unique sense of calling benefit others? You might not be feeding starving children, but your calling still impacts the world. You might not be giving shelter to the poor, but you may be solving a cultural dilemma, bringing people together, or inventing the solution to a problem deeply impacting the lives of others. Your willingness, your excellence, and your courage will touch many lives beyond your own. You may experience pleasure as you embrace your calling, but it will certainly also benefit others. Not living it isn't just a disservice to you, but is also a disservice to those you're intended to serve.

Your calling might save a child around the globe from

malnutrition, or you might teach one child how to share her lunch with a friend who's forgotten one. You might build a house to provide shelter for a family, or you might equip one woman in recovery from addiction the life skills she needs to hold her family together. You might raise millions of dollars to benefit communities, or you might help one person you see everyday gather enough money for the security deposit on an apartment. The efficacy of your calling is measured by whether you are willing to embrace the thing that has your name on it, for the benefit of others.

Your calling—that is based on your giftedness, desires, and affirmations—will always build the story of another for the purpose of benefiting the other. As author Frederick Buechner once said, "The place God calls you to is the place where your deep gladness and the world's deep hunger meet."[6] As you consider your internal sense of calling, also consider its external effects. As you consider others in this process you might just discover that your calling can satisfy a great hunger that's not your own.

ASK

How has my work benefitted others in the past? Is there a connection between what I did and how others were affected?

_____

_____

_____

_____

BELIEVE

My calling isn't for me; it's for them.

DO   ☐ COMPLETED

In order of impact, list 2-3 of your passions that offer the greatest benefit to others. Then explain the value those people will experience.

_____

_____

_____

_____

_____

_____

_____

"What you
do makes a
difference, and
you have to
decide what kind
of difference you
want to make."

JANE GOODALL

DAY 09
Calling Is Close To Home

I (Veronica) have a friend who is a social chameleon. She never seemed to be herself and, instead, adjusted to the passions of those in the room. She was so enthusiastic about life and work and serving that after listening to the other girl's conversations, she would be convinced that their calling must be hers, too.

Perhaps you've been tempted in the similar way. If your mom was a schoolteacher, you might think that you're called to work with children. If your sister went into business, you might think that has your name on it as well. While this can sometimes work out, calling must be profoundly connected to one's own talents and gifts.

I've felt this temptation myself. Because a lot of my friends are communicators—authors and bloggers and speakers—I once felt a lot of pressure to be a full-time blogger. But as I've grown more comfortable with my own calling, I've felt the freedom to let blogging simply remain a hobby.

Your calling is unique to you. Where do you excel? What gives you energy? Which skills do you possess in greater measure than most others you know? Gifts and talents are interconnected, but they are not interchangeable. Knowing the difference between the two will help you determine which of each you posses.

Talents are skills that you inherit. They come from either your parents or your extended gene pool. We probably all know someone who comes from a family with natural abilities in a particular area. Think of Venus and Serena Williams. Or actresses Zooey and Emily Deschanel. Talents are those innate skills so prominent in a family lineage that if someone doesn't have them, others may remark, "Oh, she didn't get the (fill-in-the-blank) gene." (Just what every girl loves to hear, right?)

Gifts are skills that you acquire. Like any present, a gift is received. For us spiritual folks, they're those skills you received divinely. But more commonly, gifts can also be viewed as a result of environment. You became great at art because the schools you attended had excellent art teachers who nurtured your interests. Or you had the opportunity to excel in drama or debate because you were born into a culture that valued using your voice.

Everyone has innate talents and acquired gifts. This doesn't mean you're better at these things than anyone else, only that you possess these skills in abundance. Some of your gifts and talents are readily apparent. Others are seeds requiring fertilization, watering, and pruning. Some are valued by the culture you live in, and others that may be just as important, aren't.

As you look at your genetics and your environment, notice your talents and gifts. And then ask the big question: "How might these skills shed light on what I am meant to do?"

ASK

Based on what I've seen and others have told me, what are my three most evident talents and gifts?

_____

_____

_____

_____

BELIEVE

My calling will be carried out by my natural gifting.

DO   ☐ COMPLETED

For each of your top three talents and gifts written above, list 3 areas of need where they could be utilized.

_____

_____

_____

_____

_____

_____

_____

_____

"Remember who you were before the world told you who you should be."

DANIELLE LAPORTE

#FindYourCalling

DAY 10
Remember Who You Are

Messages matter. What your parents, your teachers, your friends, your husband, or the broader culture have told you, and are still telling you, will shape your beliefs about yourself. Too often we can't hear our heart's song because there's so much noise being trumpeted by others. Today, we're going to attack three common lies of confusion and coercion that impacted the girl you used to be.

"You can't be that." Who has spoken discouragement into your life? Who spoke a 'can't' over you that haunts you at night? Maybe they've called it a 'family curse' or have told you "that's just how we [enter last name]s are." For example, when I was a kid, my neighbor's mother told her daughter that she was overweight all the time, and now this woman is convinced she is. It doesn't matter that she's thin and spends hours at the gym. She is literally killing herself to prove that she isn't fat. Maybe no one explicitly discouraged you from pursuing your calling, but if you couldn't see women you admired doing that thing that you're called to do, you might have believed it was impossible. As the Bible says, "Train a child up in the way that they should go, and they will not depart from it." (Proverbs 22:6) If you were raised with vision and possibility you'll embrace opportunities. If you were trained to question yourself, you'll do that, too. All around us are women fulfilling the messages they heard when they were being raised. Are you?

"You should be that." Are you living out someone else's dream? We have a friend who's an immigrant from a culture that encourages children to pursue 'respectable' careers like being physicians or lawyers. Today she is a doctor, but we've wondered what she'd be doing if her parents hadn't pushed her into that field. Maybe you grew up knowing that you were expected to attend college and graduate school. Or you were taught that you had to help people in a career like nursing or social work—even if those were not your callings. How many people are stuck because of the shoulds that have been spoken over them?

"You were not meant to be that." Often your calling is the very thing you've been told by someone else you can't do or would never be. You'll need to identify these comments and examine their validity. Some women were raised in homes that promoted career and success to the neglect of family. Others were raised in homes that devalued women to the point of crushing any dreams to have an impact outside the walls of their home. In order to discover your calling, you'll need to develop the discernment to evaluate your options objectively.

Finding out what we're meant to do is a beautiful mess. But to put it in the words of Dale's mentor, "Don't just remember who you were before the world told you who you should be. Remind yourself of who you were before the world told you who you can't be. And in that place is where you'll find who you are called to be."

ASK

What harmful messages have the people from my past told me? How have they affected my thinking?

_____

_____

_____

_____

BELIEVE

If I believe a lie, it will negatively affect my life.

DO   ☐ COMPLETED

Take five minutes to remind yourself who you are. Below, write down as many true things about your personality as you can think of. Start with "I am..."

_____

_____

_____

_____

_____

_____

_____

_____

"If you think wrong, you'll never live strong."

LISA JACOBSON

DAY 11
Asking The Right Questions

When it comes to calling, where you start will influence how you finish. Think of an Olympic race. You can have the most ballin' shoes and the flashiest gear and even lightning fast legs, but if you're starting 200 meters behind the other runners, it won't matter.

Unfortunately, the way many popular leaders have talked about calling hasn't been helpful. They've thrown out slick clichés that don't help us move any closer to discovering what we were meant to do. They're simply shadows of the classic childhood question, "What do you want to be when you grow up?" Our guess is that you've heard, repeated, or pondered one or two of these poorly crafted questions yourself, so let's unravel a few of them.

Incorrect Question: "If money were no object, what would you do?"

This one is so unrealistic, I'm surprised so many people suggest it. Starting with "if money were no object" is like starting with "if you didn't have to breathe air." It's not realistic because money will always be an object. If Dale and I start acting as if money doesn't matter, we'll end up in a world of trouble. While we should fear the temptations that come from excess money, as well as the perils of poverty, we can't pretend that money doesn't matter.

Correct Question: If you could choose a calling that would fuel your passions and provide for your family, what would you do?

Incorrect Question: "If you could guarantee that you wouldn't fail, what would you attempt?"

The first problem with this query is the same as the last one. You can't guarantee you will not fail. If you're willing to try something new, failure will always be a possibility. If you're 45-years-old and want to leave your teaching job to be a swimsuit model in Milan, it it probably isn't going to happen. Every woman should consider the real possibility of failure before bailing on what she's doing right. At the same time, this posture assumes that failure is negative. But there is failure that can also grow us, show us, and at times direct us toward our calling.

Correct Question: Despite the possibility of failure, what are you willing to take a risk on?

Incorrect Question: "If you could do anything, what would make you happy?"

The problem with this is that it assumes that whatever makes you happy must be good for you. If sex makes you happy, then you might as well cheat on your husband to have more of it. If money makes you happy, then you'll feel validated in your materialism. Rather than ask what makes us happy and pursue it blindly, we should ask whether the things that make us happy should make us happy. Yes, our callings should offer fulfillment and happiness. But just because something makes you happy, doesn't mean it qualifies as a 'calling.'

Correct Question: Of the things that make you happy, which are the ones that make you whole?

ASK

How can I avoid faulty arguments that can muddy my discernment about my calling?

_____

_____

_____

_____

BELIEVE

I will direct my life with wisdom, rather than through cliché aphorisms.

DO   ☐ COMPLETED

Answer the three 'correct' questions.

_____

_____

_____

_____

_____

_____

_____

_____

"The art of being wise is the art of knowing what to overlook."

WILLIAM JAMES

DAY 12
The Oversaturated Calling

I (Veronica) mentioned how I admired my friends who were bloggers. One of the greatest threats to your calling can be your fascination with someone else's. Too many people begin to explore their callings and then balk after realizing they aren't the only one who has it.

"Too many people do this," they say. "I'll never be better than the rest."

Dale struggled with this feeling when he decided to live out part of his calling by writing a book. He looked at the marketplace and saw other books on business, leadership, and entrepreneurship. A voice in his head whispered that the need was already met and he was wasting his time. The voice told him that the other authors were better than him and that the finish line had already been crossed. Why should he write a book when so many people had already written others? Who did he think he was?

The voice of shame tells men and women that we're not good enough.

In a culture where women are expected to do it all, both professionally and relationally, the search for our calling can be a prime breeding ground for fear, anxiety, and shame. So, we must deal with the internal voices that give these a foothold in our heart and minds. Three truths have helped both of us dispel these obstacles on our own journeys toward a life of purpose.

1. Fear kills calling more than failure ever will.
The path to your calling is often walked with weak knees. Everyone has a fear of failure, but many also have a fear of success. What will happen if your dream materializes, if you say yes to providing foster care, or if your online business explodes? How will you survive that level of responsibility? Do you possess the capacity, talent, and guts to operate at a higher level? Ultimately, the fear that you can't sustain your calling or survive it will often rob you of the joy of discovering it.

2. The middle road is a dead end street.
Discovering your calling requires making critical decisions. Yet many people are racked with indecision, and this creates anxiety. A friend I've (Veronica) known since childhood always wanted to be a screenwriter. She's talked about it since we were kids, and has even had the opportunity to attend conferences and seminars to gain some of the insight and skills she needs to do it. But all the pages she's written have stayed hidden away on her laptop. She's never allowed anyone else to read her words. Taking the middle road, by failing to act on her dream, led her nowhere.

Many experience 'paralysis by analysis' when they overthink a situation to the point where they end up stuck. We often assume that pausing to consider our options is a better strategy than moving forward and choosing the wrong option, but this is only true to a point. This approach eventually leads to more stress, more worry, and less serenity. Peace is found in moving, not standing still.

3. Yes, you're worthy.
When women catch a whiff of our calling, we begin to imagine how living it out will change our lives. And when the vision is better than our existing situation, we might not believe we deserve it. Bestselling author Brené Brown says, "Shame—the intensely painful feeling or experience of believing that we are flawed and therefore

87

unworthy of love and belonging—breeds fear."[7]

Some women have allowed their past to teach them that they don't deserve purpose. So they self-sabotage to prove that what they've accepted is true. Others were raised in a *quid pro quo* culture that makes them think they need to work overtime to earn whatever they get. So they self-inflict enough pain to make them feel as though they're entitled to whatever purpose they can glean.

These three barriers—fear, worry, and shame—are internal, not external. Unfortunately, it's much easier to overcome external obstacles than inner obstacles. Notice these three and scrap them. Calling is free, and everyone—including you—deserves to live with purpose.

ASK

Have I adopted patterns of faulty thinking? If so, where is the root and what can I do to begin the process of healing?

_____

_____

_____

_____

BELIEVE

I find my calling when I fix my thinking.

DO   ☐ COMPLETED

List three personal qualities of strength that will aid you in combating doubt and thinking clearly. Next, list three qualities you've not yet mastered but desire to embody.

_____

_____

_____

_____

_____

_____

_____

NOTES FOR THOUGHTS

"Knowing what must be done does away with fear."

ROSA PARKS

DAY 13

Don't Run So Fast You Leave Yourself Behind

When families go on road trips, there is always that moment when a child shouts from the back of the SUV, "Are we there yet?" (In case you were wondering, the answer is "no." If we were there, the small human would not be asking.)

Some of us act the same way. Once an idea strikes, we want the final product as soon as possible. We want to act immediately, see results, cross the finish line. We don't want to take a road trip in an SUV; we want to push a button on a teleporter.

Some not only tolerate haste, they celebrate it. They've embroidered the swag with the logo of their new Etsy shop before they've considered a business plan! They brag about how quickly they're moving, dubbing themselves "go-getters." I (Veronica) have a friend who blew through a series of failed small businesses in six years: putting family photos on video, designing cards, hocking t-shirts, beading badge lanyards, selling puppets and creating custom car magnets. She had a lot of energy, but never paused to prepare for success.

To call her a "go-getter" is to rename a flaw as an asset. Unfortunately, this kind of haste can short-circuit a journey toward purpose. These women confuse impatience with persistence. They fail to value and utilize the time between inspiration and realization as a critical period for preparation.

The value of this principle has been deeply ingrained in some of our Jewish friends. They grew up hearing about Moses spending 40 years waiting in the wilderness. They're familiar with the story of King David being called as a boy to lead, but waiting years to serve. They know the story of Daniel who spent nearly a decade serving a pagan king before his famous lion's den moment. As a Christian, we also value the wisdom of waiting. Jesus waited 30 years before launching his ministry and the Apostle Paul spent prep time in the desert after discovering his calling and before living it out.

Though it's natural to wish for immediate results like Jack and his magical beanstalk, you're not Jack and your calling isn't a beanstalk. If you've recently planted the seed in the ground, don't expect a tree to germinate, sprout, and grow overnight. Plan, instead, to work for your calling and wait for your timing. Patience isn't just a torture device; it's a shaping tool.

ASK

What role has patience played in my life? Is waiting for the long-term vision difficult for me? What will help me to patiently endure the time between inspiration and realization?

_____

_____

_____

_____

_____

_____

_____

BELIEVE

The time between now and the realization of my life's work is the most important season of my life.

DO   ☐ COMPLETED

Look up one of history's great leaders whose life inspires you, and find their biography. Whether it's the short or long version, read it. Take your time and notice the richness of the timeline, not the rush to the finish line.

"Passion is the willingness to suffer for something you love."

UNKNOWN

#FindYourCalling

DAY 14
Misery Loves Company

I (Veronica) have a friend named Jen who worked in a preschool for years. She loved it and assumed that she'd be in the education system for the rest of her life. Then she noticed an itch for more. Her marriage had a pretty rocky season, and she wanted to use her story to help others whose marriages were also struggling. Unlike others I've heard who talked about writing a book or starting a blog, Jen actually did it. Her story resonates with a lot of women and she's been extremely successful.

If Jen had continued as a preschool teacher, she might have had satisfying career. But she would have missed out on the calling that only she could fulfill. And millions of women would have missed out on the hope and healing they've received because Jen was willing to discern and pursue her calling.

As you discern your calling, others will weigh in.
Hear everyone, but only listen to a few.

People are wired to pursue calling. They want to discover it and may be frustrated if they haven't found it. So, some may be jealous when they witness you searching for yours or living it out. Although everyone has a specific purpose in this life, insecurity persuades people to behave otherwise.

The advice some offer may not be helpful. It might not sound malicious. It might not be very far off base. It might even come from a well-meaning place. But their words won't always align with what you're discovering to be true about yourself. When you notice the tension of this misalignment, exercise caution. Misery loves company, but you don't have to join the party.

Imagine what your life would look like if you always listened to what people said about who you were supposed to be or what you were supposed to do. Some advice may have been useful; other words would be better ignored.

Be willing to plug in, listen, and notice what's motivated by love, wisdom, jealousy, or brokenness. As you exercise discernment, you'll learn to recognize the truth when you hear it.

ASK

Who comes to mind when I think of the people that truly want the best for me? How have they proven they are worth listening to?

_____

_____

_____

_____

BELIEVE

Just because something sounds smart to me doesn't mean it's right for me.

DO   ☐ COMPLETED

List three non-negotiable traits that qualify someone to speak into your journey to discover your calling.

_____

_____

_____

_____

_____

_____

_____

"Discernment is the ability to see things for what they really are, not for what you want them to be."

UNKNOWN

DAY 15
Clearly Uncomfortable

Think about a moment in your life when your future was guaranteed. Keep thinking. Don't stop. Just one time. A single moment. Do you have it in your mind? We didn't think so. Your good health could evaporate tomorrow. The stock market could crash and wipe away your savings. Your husband could be involved in an accident, a loved one could tragically pass away, or your house could burn down.

Uncertainty makes us uncomfortable. When we're missing information, or when we anticipate the possibility of danger, uncertainty elicits caution. Humans naturally resist it. We plan for the future, prepare for the future, and save for the future. Yet as hard as we work hard to minimize uncertainty, we'll never eliminate it. Accepting this reality is critical to discovering what we were meant to do.

Discovering your calling requires stepping into the unknown. Walking into mystery. Relinquishing control. If ambiguous situations make you step back or shut down, you'll fail to discover your purpose. Uncertainty is a prerequisite of calling and allowing that discomfort requires courage.

Though we might feel uncertain, we shouldn't be indecisive. If you make a bad decision, people will forgive you and you can forgive yourself. But if you cannot make a decision, you'll have no traction to move forward. So, you must learn to walk with confidence into uncertain seasons of your life. There's no way to predict what you'll discover as you search for your purpose, but you can hold your head high and stand strong while you seek it out. You might not know the curve of every trail, but you can be confident that you're climbing the right mountain.

ASK

On this journey toward clarity, what scares me?

_____

_____

_____

_____

BELIEVE

Sometimes my only option for moving forward is a leap of faith.

DO   ☐ COMPLETED

List three elements of your calling about which you currently have clarity. Next, list three elements of your calling about which you feel uncertain.

_____

_____

_____

_____

_____

_____

_____

_____

_____

NOTES FOR THOUGHTS

"I'd rather regret the things I've done than regret the things I haven't done."

LUCILLE BALL

DAY 16
Let Your Life Do The Preaching

20th century British writer C.S. Lewis described the
humble man,

"Do not imagine that if you meet a really humble man
he will be what most people call 'humble' nowadays:
he will not be a sort of greasy, smarmy person, who is
always telling you that, of course, he is nobody. Probably
all you will think about him is that he seemed a cheerful,
intelligent chap who took a real interest in what you said
to him."[8]

The person Lewis describes is less interested
in attracting attention to himself than he is in
engaging with and noticing others. While it sounds

counterintuitive, being humble in your calling is the key to living your calling with boldness.

It's possible that, in the course of this journey, you've been tempted to overshare insights you're gleaning about the nature of your calling, but we've found three ways to responsibly resist that urge.

1. Accept the process.

Unwrapping a calling is like reading a book. In our early years we might glimpse some of the first pages, but not known where they were leading. We knew enough to have a general idea of the content, and a general direction the story was headed, but we didn't know how the narrative would unfold. Conversations, life lessons, and relationships eventually reveal additional sentences, paragraphs, and pages. By the time we're old, and our hair has turned grey, we'll finally have access to the entire book.

As you realize and accept that calling is a process, and that you are not the one writing the book, you'll live into and speak about your calling with more humility.

2. Don't declare your calling; display it.

Don't be that swag-embroidering girl who deciphers her calling, prints the business cards and acquires the domain name without any input or affirmation from others. Instead, simply go out and use your gift. Let people see your calling. Let people affirm your calling. Organic affirmation from a variety of sources over a long stretch of time might be the most powerful assurance one can receive. Here's the uncomfortable truth: if nobody agrees or affirms it, then it's likely not your calling. If everyone else affirms it, because you're faithfully living it out, then you won't have to do the excruciating work of convincing them.

3. Release your expectations.

We've addressed overcoming your fears and others' expectations for your journey. However, the challenge in this part of the process is relinquishing your own expectations. In a world where everyone gets a trophy and we're inundated with messages about how special we are, most of us expect to be the heroes of our own lives. We expect to succeed. We expect to have the spotlight shining brightly on our lives. Release the expectation you have to be the hero of every scene. Your calling makes you the world's servant, not the world's savior.

ASK

When I think of a humble yet confident person, what character traits come to mind?

_____

_____

_____

_____

_____

_____

BELIEVE

Humility isn't denying my strengths; it's embracing my weaknesses.

DO   ☐ COMPLETED

List three ways you can show your community your calling without telling them your calling.

_____

_____

_____

_____

_____

_____

"Humility in women has more effect than beauty."

RUTH GRAHAM

DAY 17
Pick a Road and Go

People often use the phrase "the road less travelled" to describe choosing a path or making a difficult decision that others haven't chosen. The phrase comes from a Robert Frost poem and most people overlook an important detail. The narrator looks at two paths and notes that the more traveled road looked "just as fair." In other words, both roads had their strengths and weakness, their positives and negatives, their pros and cons. One path seemed to be as good of an option as the other.

This is where most of us live when it comes to our callings. We see two possible paths forward that seem good enough. Maybe more. We have the gifts and talents and passions that would allow us to succeed in any of the several paths before us.

Maybe you're sitting at your kitchen table with your mind maps, questionnaires, index cards and post-it notes spread out in front of you. You're wondering how you're supposed to choose a path with all of this information available to you. Which road should you travel, and how should you choose?

I (Dale) once heard brilliance defined as "making something complex seem simple." So, begin by narrowing your options. Options can be a blessing, but can also be a burden. To succeed, you need to whittle down your possibilities to a manageable number of options. I suggest forcing yourself to release all but three. Keep them broad. Don't write that you want to start a summer camp; write that you want to work with youth. Don't write the name and mission statement of the non-profit you want to start; write that you want to give the world clean water.

To discern among the three, you'll need to use your intuition. Also, consider consulting some of your wisest confidants.

We're not asking you to identify a calling just yet, but to move in that direction sort your thinking into categories by using this guide:

1. List what you've discerned as your top 3 callings. (Yes, literally write them down.)

2. Add one sentence about why each direction excites you. What would you be saying 'yes' to?

3. Add another sentence about what you would be saying 'no' to if you choose a particular direction.

You may only need to follow this three-step process once to make a selection. You might try it and know that you know. But you might complete it and still feel torn. In this case, you may need to spend time thinking and praying and discerning. Or perhaps you'll need to give yourself permission to test one and see what happens. It's okay if you spend time pursuing your sense of a calling that doesn't pan out. And it's also okay that you choose not to travel every possible road. Don't worry about choosing the road least traveled; discover and take the one you feel called to walk.

ASK

Do I typically go with the flow or pave my own way?
Why do I do this?

_____

_____

_____

_____

BELIEVE

If I want to be extraordinary I must eliminate the
unnecessary.

DO   ☐ COMPLETED

Complete the exercise found in today's lesson.

_____

_____

_____

_____

_____

_____

_____

_____

"The most difficult thing is the decision to act, the rest is merely tenacity."

AMELIA EARHART

DAY 18
The Right of Passage

When people are seeking discernment, they often seek sound. They listen to a podcast or have a conversation with a likeminded friend or hire a coach to offer advice. Or maybe they read a book, which is visual sound that stimulates the brain like an audible voice.

While all of these growth techniques can be useful, sometimes we need to quiet our hearts and minds to learn through silence.

Up until now in this process, you've been receiving and processing information to clarify your calling. You've synthesized wisdom and advice through the questions and exercises in these pages. You've had vulnerable conversations in community. And you've explored the nuances of your gifts and talents. Now it's time to shut up and ship out.

Science is now revealing that silence is even more beneficial for human bodies and minds than we once assumed. A few minutes of silence can increase your blood circulation, lower your blood pressure, and promote brain cell production. You're actually more creative right after periods of silence, which is why you may get a spark of genius in the middle of the night. People who spend time in silence have lower rates of depression and anxiety. They also have longer attention spans. While you may think silence is a waste of your time, it may be one of the best ways you can spend your time.

The moment you decide to commit to your calling is a monumental one. To prepare for it, I'm asking you to enter a period of intentional quiet time to clarify your thoughts and steady your sea legs. For some, it might mean a trip to the mountains. For others it might be an overnight at the beach. Someone else might hole up in a friend's home while they're away. Whatever you choose here are a few ground rules for your pause trip:

Retreat for at least 24 hours. Jesus took 40 days and nights. If you can't set aside one day, then you're not ready to live this out. If you have children, choose someone you trust—ideally your spouse!—to come stay with your kids. Knowing they're secure is going to free you up to pay attention to what's going on inside of you.

Relinquish technology. Your phone and laptop need to stay shut down. And, I'm sorry, but you'll have to miss The Bachelor. No television. You have to disconnect to reconnect.

Get outside if possible. Humans are meant to connect with nature. It is our natural habitat. So, leave the phosphorescent glow of your home and explore the outdoors.

Choose a quiet place. I (Veronica) find being near a lake or river rejuvenating. But your sacred spot could be a cabin, a cottage or maybe just a hotel room. Whatever it is, it must be quiet.

During your getaway, spend as much time in quiet as possible. Think. Pray. Journal. Daydream. Clear the distractions so that you can discover for yourself:

You are not stuck.
You are moving forward.
You don't yet know how you'll get there.
You're doing the necessary hard work to figure it out.
You're ready to accept your calling and live what you were meant to do.

ASK

Where does my best thinking occur? How can I integrate this into my pause trip?

_____

_____

_____

_____

BELIEVE

Silence is an important ingredient to discover my calling.

DO   ☐ COMPLETED

Schedule the date for your pause trip and fill in the details below.

_____

_____

_____

_____

_____

_____

_____

"Thousands of tired, nerve-shaken, over-civilized people are beginning to find out that going to the mountains is going home; that wildness is a necessity."

JOHN MUIR

#FindYourCalling

DAY 19
Breaking Ground

I (Veronica) mentioned I'm an animal person, but my love for birds is left out of that statement. I don't mind hearing them, or looking at them, but I don't want to touch one. Ever. Seriously, I'd rather have a spider crawl on me than to be touched by a bird.

In our experience, men and women have different fears. Among men's greatest worries is the fear of making a bad decision. What if you hire the wrong person? Or what if you fire the wrong person? What if you miscalculate a financial decision that puts your family at risk? Women, though, often fear making a decision that ruptures relationships. Because we value our bonds with others, we worry about making a choice that threatens those we care about.

But failing to make a decision can also jeopardize what each of us values most.

At this point in the journey to discover and embrace your calling, you have enough information to determine what you were meant to do. You've thought about it, prayed about it, and talked to others about it. You've made lists and taken inventory. You've been wise, patient, and thorough. If you've still not been able to determine at least the general direction, fear is what's holding you back or slowing you down.

This is the moment to notice what your default behavior is. Are you always playing it safe? Are you too impulsive? Do you procrastinate? Notice whether there might be a persistent behavior hindering your journey. Ask those around you what hampers your ability to make a confident decision. Call it out, let it go, and move forward.

If this advice seems simplistic, it is. Once you've done all the necessary work needed to make a good choice, nothing is left to do but to make it. If you are too fearful to inch forward, you'll have to release that fear before you can move on. If you refuse to release it, you'll stay stuck. At this point, no one can help you except you.

Only you can overcome the paralysis that's kept you stuck.

Accepting a calling doesn't mean you've forever sealed your fate. Be open to change, but commit to move in the direction you've chosen. You'll evolve over time, just like a sapling that becomes a tree—especially if your life circumstance, like marriage or children, changes. But you'll need to emerge from the ground in order to begin the process. You can't start growing until you get going.

ASK

What's stopped me, in the past, from making big decisions? Are those same elements at play here?

_____

_____

_____

BELIEVE

I won't fear the consequence of my choice more than the result of not choosing at all.

DO   ☐ COMPLETED

Produce the first draft of your calling in words.
I'm called to: [1-3 sentence version]
I'm called to: [Five words or less version.]

_____

_____

_____

_____

_____

_____

_____

_____

"I learned a long time ago that there is something worse than missing the goal, and that's not pulling the trigger."

MIA HAMM

DAY 20
Passion, Meet Preparation

You're getting ready to launch into one of life's great adventures. So, you might be thinking that you need a little bit of luck right about now. Should you purchase a rabbit's foot? Ask your pastor to anoint you with special oil? Eat a bowl of Lucky Charms? (They are magically delicious, after all.)

We don't believe that any of these steps are necessary. As entrepreneur and bestselling author Jack Canfield has said, "People make their own luck by great preparation and good strategy." Show me the luckiest business leader who changed the world, and I'll show you a prepared leader with a solid plan.

What do you need to do in order to fully embrace your calling? Some will need to create a list of tasks. Others need to down a list of pros and cons. Some need to have some more conversations with trusted mentors. Others may need to write letters to themselves. And others may need to enlist professional assistance to help them move forward.

No matter who you are, you need to draft a plan. As with drafting a business plan, many people assume that this process is for the benefit of others. But this is actually for you. While your day of silence equipped your heart, drafting your plan will equip your head. Passion is helpful, but so is preparation.

Let's start with a two-page calling overview. This will be the final document that defines your calling, and it is the proof—to yourself and to others—that you've done your homework before moving forward.

Two-page calling overview

1. Short overview of my calling:
One sentence

2. Long overview of my calling:
One paragraph

3. A list of fears I will need to overcome:
At least 5

4. A list of possibilities about which I am excited:
At least 5

5. A list of the confidants I've sought advice from:
List friends, families, and spiritual advisors here

6. A summary of the feedback I received from confidants:
A few paragraphs max

7. A list of the professionals I've consulted with:
List coaches, competitors, or collaborators in your industry here

8. A summary of the feedback I received from professionals:
A maximum of a few paragraphs

9. The season I am currently in and what that means to me:
Pick one: discovering, training, or operating

10. Here is the first step I plan to take to live my calling:
2-3 sentences

11.Here is the shape I hope my calling will take in 5 years:
One paragraph

You are welcome to take time to think and pray over this, but no more than 48 hours. Any more means you're probably procrastinating. It's time to start living your calling. Everyone is waiting.

ASK

Am I a natural planner? If yes, what benefits have I seen from it? If no, what consequences have I seen because of it?

_____

_____

_____

_____

_____

_____

_____

_____

_____

_____

BELIEVE

If I fail to plan, I'm planning to fail.

DO   ☐ COMPLETED

Write your two page calling overview, print it, and keep accessible for easy viewing.

NOTES FOR THOUGHTS

"Discipline is doing things we don't necessarily like to achieve the things we love."

JASON BENHAM

#FindYourCalling

DAY 21
Your Life's Work

Happiness expert Gretchen Rubin says there are four stages to enjoying a happy event. (And we'd call discovering your calling a happy event!) The first stage is "anticipation." You've been looking forward to finding your calling for days, weeks, months, and maybe years.

But now that you've found, accepted and committed to your calling, you can begin working through the next ones. Step two is "savoring," which means enjoying the moment. This journey you've embarked on is worth celebrating, so plan something big.

Step three is "expressing," which means sharing the joy with others. Help your friends, family, and coworkers discover and embark on the journey you've just completed.

Step four is "reflecting," which means looking back on the happy time you've enjoyed. Social media, a natural documentation of our lives, may help you review where you've been. As you embrace your calling, be intentional to take photos and mark important moments along the way.

You haven't just unlocked your calling. You've also unlocked personal fulfillment and happiness. Why? Because not only have you started living the first three steps, but you've started the process all over. Accepting your calling means you have given yourself something to anticipate again.

As you reach for the mountain top—that pinnacle that is your life's work—you're going to continue to grow in accomplishments. This may not happen immediately, but it will happen. Josephine Cochrane invented the electric dishwasher when she was 48. Maya Angelou read her poem "On the Pulse of Morning" at the inauguration of President Bill Clinton when she was 65. George Burns received his Oscar at 80. So, be patient. You've got a long voyage ahead of you.

And don't forget that the goal isn't the destination, but the journey. You're going to be learning, growing, and expanding along the way as you begin pursuing your life's work.

In just 21 days, you've done the hard work of finding the right road for your life. This is something worth celebrating.

ASK

What has this process revealed to me that I never expected?

_____

_____

_____

_____

_____

_____

_____

_____

_____

_____

BELIEVE

The most fortunate people on earth are those who have found their calling.

DO   ☐ COMPLETED

Go start your new life.

"The goal isn't the destination, it's the journey."

UNKNOWN

FINAL STEPS
And Fun Suggestions

As you pursue your true calling, keep a few things in mind. Sometimes we imagine that doing what we're meant to do will feel easy. It's simply not true. Calling is hard work. Really hard work. There will even be seasons of what feels like dead work. You will still have days when you won't feel like embracing your calling and even days when you want to quit. Such is the nature of all work.

One of my (Veronica) favorite statements comes from the sixth chapter of the book of Galatians, "Let us not lose heart in doing good, for in due time we will reap if we do not grow weary."

Your good work will never be done in vain. It will be work that expands instead of constricts your spirit, leaving you feeling more, not less, alive. It will be work that stretches you, grows you, and helps you reach your potential as a woman. It will be work that satisfies not only your hunger, but a hunger in the world. Most of all, it will give you the incomparable feeling that there is a reason and purpose for your existence. It confirms that you are where you are meant to be, doing what you were meant to do.

Before we leave you, we want to offer you a few more resources for your journey.

1. Launch Your Dream
Launch your Dream is the title of the sequel to this book. For those who are built to work for themselves, it's the next natural step in the progression toward the realization of your life's work. While this book was a short self-published book (just under 13,000 words), Launch Your Dream is a traditionally published book with Thomas Nelson. It's 40,000 words designed as a 30-day guide for turning your passion into your profession. In terms of practical advice for chasing a dream, Dale would call it his life's greatest work. You can pick up a copy at StartupCamp.com/Launch

2. StartupCamp.com
For those looking for a more hands-on guide to self-

employment, freelancing, or launching your own business, join the over 250,000 monthly readers of Dale's blog and the over 2,000 students enrolled in his 12-month step-by-step program at StartupCamp.com

3. The StartupCamp Podcast

There's a reason Dale's show is a top 100 leadership and business podcast on iTunes. Each week he interview bestselling authors, thriving entrepreneurs, and others who are among the most successful people on the planet (many of which are women). Join over 100,000 monthly listeners for a show that will not only strengthen your professional life but will inspire your personal life, too. Simply open up your podcast app on your phone or listen online at StartupCamp.com/Podcast

As you may have noticed, I'm not the biggest user of social media but you can join the over 1 million people who follow Dale's daily posts for creating the business and family you love.

To a lovely life of purpose,

Veronica & Dale Partridge

Follow Veronica

- VeronicaPartridge.com/Facebook
- VeronicaPartridge.com/Instagram
- VeronicaPartridge.com/Pinterest

Follow Dale

- Facebook.com/DaleJPartridge
- Instagram.com/DalePartridge
- Twitter.com/DalePartridge
- Pinterest.com/DalePartridge

END NOTES
For Your Reference

1. https://www.sharecare.com/health/eye-vision-health/vision-different-for-men-women

2. John Donne, Devotions Upon Emergent Occasions, (New York: Oxford University Press, 1987), 103-110.

3. Jeanne Meister, "Job Hopping Is the 'New Normal' for Millennials: Three Ways to Prevent a Human Resource Nightmare," Forbes, August 14, 2012, accessed October 9, 2016, http://www.forbes.com/sites/jeannemeister/2012/08/14/job-hopping-is-the-new-normal-for-millennials-three-ways-to-prevent-a-human-resource-nightmare/#1d5ff4b85508.

4. Katharine Brooks Ed.D., "Job, Career, Calling: Key to Happiness and Meaning at Work?," Psychology Today, June 29, 2012, accessed October 12, 2016, https://www.psychologytoday.com/blog/career-transitions/201206/job-career-calling-key-happiness-and-meaning-work.

5. Brett and Kate McKay, "Finding Your Calling Part 1," The Art of Manliness, May 24, 2010, accessed September 22, 2016, http://www.artofmanliness.com/2010/05/24/finding-your-calling-part-i-what-is-a-vocation/.

6. Frederick Buechner, Wishful Thinking: A Seeker's ABC (New York: HarperOne, 1993)

7. Brené Brown, I Thought It Was Just Me (But It Isn't!): Making the Journey from "What Will People Think?" to "I Am Enough" (New York: Penguin, 2007).

8. C.S. Lewis, Mere Christianity. (New York, New York: HarperOne, 2015), p. 128.

TURN YOUR CALLING INTO YOUR CAREER.

BUILD A BUSINESS THAT CHANGES THE WORLD

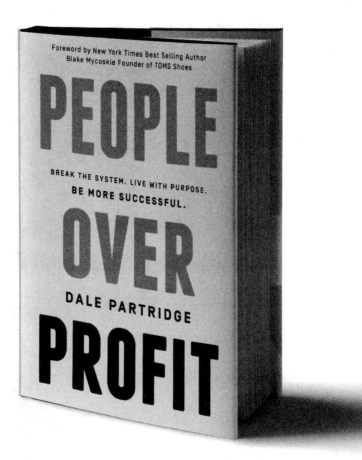

Foreword by New York Times Best Selling Author
Blake Mycoskie Founder of TOMS Shoes

PEOPLE

BREAK THE SYSTEM. LIVE WITH PURPOSE.
BE MORE SUCCESSFUL.

OVER

DALE PARTRIDGE

PROFIT

StartupCamp.com/People

DO YOU HAVE A BUSINESS IDEA BUT DON'T KNOW WHERE TO BEGIN?

Enroll in Dale Partridge's
12-month coaching course

- Coching Videos
- PDF Packs
- Study Guides
- Checklists

- Training Articles
- Podcasts
- Video Interviews
- Live Call Q&A's

Create the business and life you love.

⊙ StartupCamp.com

NOTES FOR THOUGHTS

_____

_____

_____

_____

_____

_____

_____

_____

_____

_____

_____

_____

_____

_____

_____

_____

_____

_____

NOTES FOR THOUGHTS

NOTES FOR THOUGHTS